"Come, my cubs," said Vixen, "While you is out hunting each night, I shall teach you about the creatures of the Charnwood and how to treat them."

Her cubs finished suckling and lay around their mother, as she told them the first story.

"Tonight," she said, "I will tell you of Hares and Rabbits.

Rabbits and Hares are, of course, a staple diet for Foxes.  But by Fox law, you must never hunt Rabbits on the Warren Hills."

"Why not?" asked a fluffy, inquisitive cub.

"I should have expected you to ask," laughed Vixen. "The reason is one of Fox Honour, and that is, of course, the *MOST* important cause. Even the Guardians will think twice of coming between a fox and its honour.

"Now our tale begins over 100 years ago, before the monks came. At this time, the hill, which is now known as 'the Calvary', was known as 'Kite Hill'.

"I have told you about the Buzzards and Owls that still hunt on the Charnwood. And told you that while you are still cubs, you must keep an eye on the sky lest you become a bird's dinner. Well, the Kites were worse!

"Buzzards and Owls hunt alone, and even they are a danger to a cub. Kites often hunted in groups and shared the kill. A young Fox would be a tempting treat, and back in those days, Foxes lived in fear of them.

"We Foxes hunt best at dusk and dawn; we have no choice. Imagine my children, a young, inexperienced fox out on the open shrubland around the tors of the Warren Hills, unaware that she is being watched by a whole colony of Kites.

"They would wait for her to pick up a scent, and as her attention is focused on following it

# Tales of the Charnwood.

(As told by a vixen of good breeding.)

By Constantine

Published in the United Kingdom by

Coalville C.A.N. Community Publishing
Memorial Square,
Coalville,
Leicestershire,
England
LE67 3TU

First Published in 2025
First Edition

10 9 8 7 6 5 4 3 2 1
Https://coalvilleccp.uk

# Foreword
## By Ghaz'on the Goblin

Since I first wrote down the adventures of Bailey and Scruff, there has been much interest in the lore of the Charnwood. I understand that even some Humans have read these stories though I find it hard to believe.

But I thought it might be nice to recount some genuine folk tales which were told to me by a Vixen of good standing and I present them here as she told them to her cubs.

## A note on the text:

Human languages are very strange, and I have done my best.

In English word man is not capitalised, but Welshman, or Frenchman, is, because it talks about specific groups of people. But on the Charnwood the difference between Foxes and Rabbits is the same to us as the difference between say Englishmen and Scotsmen are for you. So, I have done my best.

I hope you enjoy it.

Yours,

Ghaz'on.

and finding her breakfast, the Kites take silently to the air, sweeping over the ground, their sharp talons spread out. Then, each in turn, the Kites would tear into the fox and dart away before it could react.

"Instead of finding a meal, the fox would be one."

"But what about the Rabbits?" said one of the cubs.

"Calm down, and I will tell you the story," she said, and she did.

***

One day, a Fox went out to hunt. Although he wasn't the youngest of Foxes, he was still quite inexperienced. As he hunted, feeling reasonably safe under the cover of the rowans and oaks, he caught a whiff on the breeze of hare.

Ahh, the taste of hare, far better than a rabbit, as every Fox knows; but you won't find Hares under a tree. The Fox checked the breeze and

slowly and silently made his way over the open ground towards the irresistible scent of a still snoozing hare.

As he approached his prey, the Kites attacked. The hare saw them before it saw The Fox and darted away, the Fox sprang after it, causing the leading Kite's attack to miss, though its talon raked the Fox's thigh.

The Fox howled and limped off towards the nearest cover, the Warren Hills. The hares sleeping in the short grass leapt up and ran in all directions, confusing the kites, who started going after targets of opportunity.

The lead bird had the Fox's scent and was soon chasing it over the open ground. The Fox was fast, but the kite was faster, and the Fox was limping heavily on its back leg. It managed to dodge a few attacks, however now the ground was rising, and the kite was coming in for another attack. He saw a rabbit hole to his left and jumped inside.

\*\*\*

Vixen paused and looked over her children.

"Now it's important to know that while we may eat Rabbits, we Foxes never go into rabbit warrens."

"Why not?" asked several cubs. "Think of all that tasty food." Vixen laughed,

"Foxes hunt with their noses, my children and Rabbits have sharp paws.  When we catch Rabbits in the open, we usually attack from behind. In a rabbit warren, the Rabbits will fight back. When they do, they will attack our noses with their powerful feet. A fox with an injured nose won't survive.

There is only one rabbit hole you should ever jump into, and only if your life is in danger. If ever you do, never attack the Rabbits.  Talk to them, pass the time of day with them, but no matter what your instincts tell you to do, *NEVER* hurt them. And before you ask why, I'll continue the tale."

***

The Fox collapsed in the rabbit warren not far from the entrance. Outside, the Kite cried in frustration and poked its beak into the rabbit hole, but the Fox was too far inside. The Fox was in a bad way; the gash on its thigh was still bleeding, and he didn't even have enough room to lick the wound.  He lay there panting, and

after a few minutes, he heard movement further down the tunnel, then voices.

"Smells like a fox," said the loudest voice. "Remember, back paws... attack the face, especially the end of the nose."

"Please, don't attack," the Fox called out. "I am no threat; in fact, I think I might be dying."

"Well, that may be the case, or it may not," said the voice in the passage, "If you are dying, then you can jolly well do it outside."

"I can't go outside," said the Fox, "I can't turn round, and there are Kites out there waiting to finish me off."

"You are a fox," said the voice in the hall. "Foxes are our greatest enemy. You can't stay here."

The Fox was desperate now. It growled and tried to move but howled in pain. Further down the tunnel, the Rabbits were in conference.

"If it dies in our passageway, it may cause disease. We will have to block off the whole road," said one.

"Do we have to let it die?" said another.

"Foxes may be Rabbits' greatest enemy elsewhere," said a third, "here on the tors, Kites are our greatest threat, and the enemy of my enemy is my friend."

The voices in the tunnel went on for some time, and the Fox passed out. When he woke, there was grass over his wound, and the bleeding had stopped. A great rabbit stood in front of him, its pink eyes seemed to glow red in the light which filtered in from the tunnel entrance.

"Good," the Rabbit said, "you're awake."

"Yes," said the Fox, "I'm surprised. I thought I was done for."

"We have stopped the bleeding," said Rabbit, "now you just need rest and water..."

"I might as well wish for the moon," said the Fox.

"No," said the Rabbit. "You just need to make a promise on Fox Honour."

Another voice reached the Fox's ears at this point, from just inside the entrance of the rabbit hole. It was the unmistakable voice of a cat, and not just any cat, a Guardian no less.

"I am here on behalf of the Rabbits to listen to any agreement made," said the Guardian. "Though I promise that I favour no side over the other."

The Fox took a moment to take it in. Fox Honour was sacred, and no fox could break it, but foxes were sly and often left holes in their agreements. No doubt that's why the Guardian was there.

"I am a young fox," the Fox said, "and am still in the den of my family. Could my mother speak on my behalf?"

"Your mother has been contacted," said the Guardian, "but she says she trusts you and the family will honour any agreement you make."

The Fox sighed.

"What do you want and what do you offer?" he said at last.

The leader of the Rabbits looked at the Fox with a toothy smile.

"What we offer is a little room further down the tunnel, it has soft grass and a trickle of water in the corner, which should allow you to recover your strength. We will give you and your kind leave to use it at need from now, until the end of all Rabbits."

"Generous," said the Fox, "and you have me at a disadvantage; I can hardly disagree if I want to live. What do you ask in return?"

"We want your kind to stop eating our kind," said the chief Rabbit.

The Fox laughed, but it turned into a wince of pain.

"I can't make that promise for all of my kind," said the Fox. "I'm not sure I can even make that promise for myself. All creatures must eat. While I live in fear of the Kites, I can't blame them for what they do."

There was an uncomfortable silence in the tunnel. The Guardian broke it.

"This is where you must negotiate," said the Guardian. "The Fox cannot speak for all Foxes just as you cannot speak for all Rabbits. But he can speak for the Foxes of Charnwood, and you can speak for the Rabbits of the Warren Hills."

"That's doable," said the Fox, "I can promise on Fox Honour. That no fox of the Charnwood will hunt Rabbits on the Warren Hills from now till the end of our line."

The old Rabbit walked back and forth anxiously.

"Foxes often move to new areas. What if another fox family moves in?" asked the Rabbit.

"If they move into our territory, well... they would have to either destroy our family or join it," said the Fox, "If they destroy us, there is nought we can do. If they join us, they will have to uphold our honour. In the same token, any rabbit from your family who puts a paw outside the Warren Hills is fair game, so you must be careful."

"Agreed," said the Rabbit.

"Agreed," said the Guardian.

The Fox chuckled.

"What's so funny?" asked the Rabbit.

"Well, my family have never been much into Rabbits anyway. We much prefer the taste of hare," said the Fox, and as grim as it may seem, all three laughed.

***

Vixen looked over her cubs.

"That is why you must never hunt Rabbits on the Warren Hills," she said. "There may not be

Kites on the Calvary Tor anymore, but a deal is a deal, and the Rabbits have always upheld their side."

"Can Rabbits really talk?" asked a cub.

"All creatures can talk to some degree," said Vixen. "The more intelligent the creature and the more social the creature, the better it can talk and the better it can be understood. Hares can say little more than 'run'. But it must be said that if the Foxes on the Charnwood are pickier about who and what they eat. We are better foxes for it. Good night, my children."

And the cubs snuggled up against their mother and passed into gentle dreams.

## Chapter Two:
## Mice.

"Hurry up," said Vixen, "Tonight I shall tell you about Mice."

Her cubs finished suckling and lay around their mother. Once they were settled, she began.

*** 

Jed P'noo, the chief spokes-mouse scurried down a long golden corridor. He stopped at a little door and pushed a small button on the wall. A moment later, the door opened. The mouse took a deep, steadying breath and then stepped out into the grand audience chamber.

The chamber was huge. Even for the creatures who built and designed it, it was a massive venture. The Mice had never been intended to perform the functions now asked of them; alas, they had no choice.

Jed scurried up to the first step and looked up. From this angle, the little creature could make out the top of the Queen's great headdress. Her mighty purrs filled the hall with a deep throbbing.

The mouse struggled up the first step and stopped, panting. From here, the mouse could see the Queen's ears, which seemed to twitch ever so slightly. He scrambled up the next step as quietly as he dared; to wake the Queen at any time was to risk death. But today was no ordinary day. As he reached the penultimate step, a colossal furry paw appeared over the edge, and great retractable claws stretched out and grasped lazily at nothing before withdrawing back from whence they came.

Jed reached the top step. Four slave-mice stood around, each holding a large fan on a stick, which they beat rhythmically to keep the Queen cool. The spokes-mouse nodded to the slave nearest the Queen's head and took over his fanning duties. Silently, the other mice put down their fans and headed for the door. Though their paws made only the slightest sound on the tiled

floor, still the Queen's ears swivelled, and her claws twitched. As soon as the other Mice were out of the door, he started counting down in his head.  From forty-five down to zero. Perhaps missing the cooling air of the other fans, the Queen began shifting in her sleep. The little mouse considered running; maybe he would get lucky and make it to the device in time, however, old as she was, the Queen was fast.

'No...' he decided, 'I must stick to the plan. At least if I die, the others can escape.'

"Excuse me, your majesty," said Jed.

The Queen opened a lazy eye, the outer lid followed shortly by the inner lid, then the pupil swivelled, locked on the mouse.

"Jed P'noo!" the Queen cried, "Where are my fan slaves? I want a snack."

"I... I am sorry, they are all awaiting you in a royal procession," said Jed, "The day has come at last."

The cat's other eye opened, and suddenly the Queen was fully awake.

"They have found it at last?" she asked. "The way back to Earth?"

"They have indeed, your majesty," said Jed, "The way is open as we speak."

The Queen smiled and her teeth, white and sharp, caught the light of the torches on the walls.

"At last," she said, "I will have my revenge."

The great cat stretched, yawned, and sprang lightly down the steps. Jed P'noo scurrying clumsily after her.

"I will want a few of your fittest and healthiest warriors to volunteer," said the Queen, "I need to eat before I leave."

"But surely, when you reach Earth, there will be plenty of dumb Mice to eat?" Jed said, his voice pleading. The Queen growled.

"You and your people were brought here for food," said the Queen of the Cats. "You would be nothing if I hadn't raised you up. Bestowed intelligence upon you. Gifted you with language. I am not just your Queen; I am your GOD."

Jed gulped and followed.

"If you would like to hunt, there are some excellent specimens in the Maze," said Jed.

"Yes," the Queen said, admiring her claws, "A hunt would be good. Have everything prepared to take me to Earth when I am finished."

The Queen turned off from the main corridor, taking the stairs down to the Maze. The little mouse rushed off as fast as it could until it reached the laboratory.

To look at it from the mouse's point of view, one might have thought it was an observatory. The telescope here though was not for looking at the stars. It amplified the sunlight onto a spot just above a pool of water. Several mice were rushing around it.

"She's gone down to the Maze, how are you doing?" Jed squeaked.

"Half have gone through. We had to pause; the equipment is overheating," said one of the mouse technicians.

"We need to get everyone through," said Jed, "the Maze won't hold her long."

***

The Queen sniffed the air and followed the faintest scent. Though surrounded by rotting mouse corpses from thousands of years of feasting, the stench could not block the scent of living prey.

As she stalked, the Queen's thoughts returned, as they often did, to those who betrayed her. A thousand years at least had passed, and on this world the years were slow. How many thousands of years had passed on Earth, she couldn't even guess. Once she had been revered as a god on many worlds. Her people had loved her, a wise and just Queen, they wished for her to rule forever and here on this world they found the means to make it happen. Strange energies which were, shaped and twisted by her royal headpiece bestowed on her life eternal. For the longest time all seemed well. But then there were mutterings against her.

A cruelty came into her decisions, and a coldness. When she ordered the Maze built and for live prey to be put in it, some thought nothing of it, after all, Cats must eat. They ignored the cruelty of the request for they loved their Queen.

When Kapol-Tok refused the transport of live creatures for food through their pools. The Queen spoke of taking Kapol-Tok for herself. 'For nowhere should Cats be denied' she had pronounced. By betrayal Kapol-Tok got wind of her plans and they were cut off.

For the next thousand years the Mice were bred and trained until they could be used for simple tasks, when not being used for food. Many Cats were openly against this. By training Mice, they should also treat them with respect, the Queen cared not. With Kapol-Tok closed to her, she had all her scientists work on getting back to Earth.

Eventually they had succeeded in creating a machine which could bend the same strange energies that gave the Queen eternal life.

Focusing them onto a pool of water, and creating a portal, back to the Earth.

Instead of telling the Queen, the Cats all rushed through, blowing up the machine behind them.

***

"What happened to the cats who came back to Earth?" asked Brush, a cub whose tail was exceedingly bushy.

"Some say that in time, they became the Guardians we know of today," said Vixen, "but that is not a tale for tonight. Now settle down and let me finish the story."

***

Now there was just the Queen and the Mice. For the next few hundred years she controlled them most cruelly. She forced them to learn more until they were no different to you or I, with names and hopes and dreams of their own. They could even speak (well squeak), a crude version of Cat. Then she tasked them with rediscovering the

technology that could get her back to Earth and her revenge.

For hundreds of years, they learnt and experimented. The Queen used the Maze as a punishment. Mice that couldn't learn enough to help with the quest, were put in the Maze. Mice that disagreed with her were put in the Maze. Mice she simply didn't like the look of were put in the Maze. And when she ate them, she took her time.

The Queen shook herself out of her memories and back to the present. Something was wrong. She had been following the smell of live Mice for some time, yet the scents were getting weaker. She knew the Maze well and there were dead ends ahead. No way a live mouse could escape her. 'The smells could be pumped down through air holes,' she thought, 'I've been tricked.' She turned round and sped back the way she had come.

\*\*\*

In the laboratory, Jed was the last to escape. Before him the pool of water floated in the air, spinning and glowing. In the centre he could see Earth, and a far green space.

He moved the final switches into place, setting a brief timer on the circuits that would destroy the laboratory; at that moment the Queen burst in. It was a close race; Jed reached the already shrinking pool first and leapt through.

The hole was too small for the Queen. She put her paw through groping for the mouse but pulled it back yowling in pain. She looked at her paw. It was old and bony. The forces that made her immortal here would not work on Earth. She was trapped. A moment later the pool closed forever as the laboratory exploded.

\*\*\*

"The descendants of those Mice still live here on the Charnwood," said Vixen to her cubs. "But Mice are one of the creatures that Foxes live on.

# Mice

"Therefore, it is the law on the Charnwood that if you catch a mouse, you must ask it its name, and if it answers you must let it go because only intelligent Mice can talk."

"But why?" asked a cub. "We're much bigger than them."

"Because we live on the Charnwood," said Vixen, "and the Charnwood is a strange place where all good creatures must work together."

Even as she spoke the cubs curled up snug and warm against her and fell asleep.

# Chapter 3:
# Squirrels.

The following night, the cubs were allowed out for the first time.  They played and barked near the den while their father watched on and Vixen had a chance to hunt.

The cubs were tired out by the time Vixen returned and fed them, but even so they wouldn't settle down without a story.

As Vixen was tired out, Fox decided to help.

"Just a quick story tonight," he said. "Now your mother has been telling you what creatures you can eat and where you can and can't hunt.  So tonight, I will tell you about Squirrels."

The cubs got themselves all snuggled up against Vixen's side and Fox began.

## Squirrels

You will rarely see a live squirrel. For they wake up when we are about to go to bed and go to bed about the time we are starting to wake up.

Once in a blue moon you may see a live one on the forest floor and it's very tempting to try to hunt them. If you take my advice, you will simply ignore them and go about your business.

Now before any of you ask why, I'll tell you.

Firstly: You are very unlikely to catch one. Their senses are so sharp, it must seem like we are moving in slow motion to them.

Secondly: After you fail to catch it, it will sit up in a tree where you can't reach it and laugh at you; then it will follow you around up in the trees shouting and warning all the other creatures that you are there.

Sometimes they may even decide to make your life a waking nightmare. They will wait in the trees near your den every night, and make sure all the local creatures know when you're up and about. If that happens you will have to

stay in your den until the Squirrels are all asleep, and then you may have missed dusk, our favourite hunting time.

Thirdly: If you do manage to catch one and eat it, you will have every squirrel in the neighbourhood after you. But they won't just come after you, anyone you share a den with will be fair game; you may end up having to move.

There is a fourth reason: They are good for the forest.

Squirrels you see are ancient, far older than us foxes. They have been on this planet before even the ancestors of the foxes were around. They are older even than the Guardians.

They can't move through Dream-Space like Guardians, disappear like Brownies, or fly like Fairies; in fact, there is nothing magical about them at all. Still, they are fast and they are wise.

Many years ago, a different breed of Squirrels lived here. These Squirrels lived up in the tops of

trees and kept nuts in stores. The humans hunted them in what they called a 'cull' much as they do with Badgers and us Foxes.

It's just an excuse to kill.

There used to be Wolves and Bears on the Charnwood, Humans killed all of them, too.

Now when the old, 'red' Squirrels were killed the 'grey' Squirrels took over. They are a little different. They bury their nuts and seeds and often in this way help new trees to grow. This sustains the forest, which we all depend upon.

But now humans are trying to pretend the 'grey' Squirrels are the reason there are no 'reds' and want to start squirrel culling all over again.

They don't even eat them. It's just killing for no good reason.

So, respect the Squirrels and the forest will respect you.

\*\*\*

"Of course, sometimes you will come across a dead one," said Vixen, "and if it smells okay, help yourself, they are quite tasty."

# Chapter Four:
## Badgers.

The following evening, Vixen sat at the mouth of the den watching her cubs play for a few safe pre-dawn hours. She noticed that some of her darling children were teasing the smallest cub. Every family has someone who is the smallest, just as someone must be the biggest. Being a fox of the Charnwood, Vixen knew right from wrong and made plans to teach her cubs the difference.

She had a good store of stories at her command and soon remembered one that would suffice.

The story of the Friendly Badger.

Once her cubs had come back inside and had finished suckling, she began.

"Now dear ones, I will tell you a story of a Badger. Some Badgers are okay in their own way, some have even been known to share a den with

a fox and even be on talking terms; however, these are few and far between.

"Generally speaking, Badgers are grumpy and aggressive and quite scary, even when they're on friendly terms, except for one. This is the story of the Friendly Badger."

***

A long time ago in the quiet of the forest, a litter of Badgers was born. As with every family, there was a biggest and a smallest; but while the smallest had a small body, he had the biggest heart.

He wasn't so good at the rough-and-tumble games his siblings liked to play. He much preferred to sniff flowers, watch the stars, or talk to any creatures he happened to meet.

His own brothers and sisters were the first to tease him for his size and poor skill in wrestling contests. So, bit by bit, he started to avoid his siblings. Feeling lonely, he tried to make friends with the other night-time forest dwellers.

One night, he met a fox going about its business.

"Hello," said the Friendly Badger, "how are you?"

"Are you talking to me?" said the fox.

"Yes," said the Friendly Badger, "I'm hoping we can be friends."

The fox laughed at him.

"You can't be a real Badger. Real Badgers aren't friendly. You must be a rat with white stripes."

And from that night on every time the fox saw him, he would delight in saying something cruel.

On another night, the Badger came across a bat darting from tree to tree eating tiny insects.

"Hello," said the Friendly Badger, "how are you?"

"Are you talking to me?" said the bat.

"Yes," said the Friendly Badger, "I'm hoping we can be friends."

"Is this some sort of joke?" laughed the bat. "You're more like a stripy bunny rabbit."

And from that day on, whenever the bat saw the Friendly Badger, he would laugh at him and make up new insults.

The Friendly Badger started to feel that maybe nobody would like him. Then, one evening, sitting on his own watching the stars, he heard a snuffling in the bushes. A moment later, a head appeared under the lower leaves; it was a young hedgehog.

"Hello," said the hedgehog, "what sort of creature are you?"

"I'm a badger," said the Friendly Badger. "Would you like to be friends?"

"Oh yes," said the hedgehog. "Do you like hide-and-seek?"

"Yes," said the Friendly Badger, "it's one of my favourite games, but I've never had anyone to play with."

In no time at all, the pair were playing merrily and agreed to meet up the following night.

The next evening, when the Friendly Badger arrived at the meeting place, he was surrounded by a crowd of adult Hedgehogs, their spines quivering with anger. They shouted at him and

chased him away, warning that they would hurt him if he came near their children again.

Every creature the Friendly Badger met hurt and rejected him. He didn't understand why. He meant no harm to anyone, and yet everyone hurt him.

That autumn, he dug a new home, (which for Badgers is called a sett) just for himself and went to sleep dreaming about all the horrible things people had said to him.

Now, when animals like Badgers hibernate, they often grow, and when he emerged in the spring, he had gone from being the smallest to one of the biggest Badgers the Charnwood had ever seen.

He was no longer the 'Friendly Badger'.

In the long winter, dreaming of all the horrid things those other creatures had said and done to him, his heart had frozen and would never thaw again. He sought out everyone who used to

tease and bully him, and, one by one... he ate them.

But even then, when those who had teased him were gone, and no creature dared come near, the horrible names stayed with him. He spent the rest of his days lonely, sad, and angry.

***

"You see, children," said the Vixen, pausing just long enough to make her cubs uncomfortable.

"When you bully someone, everybody loses."

# Chapter Five:
## Rats.

"Rat again," said Fox as he laid out dinner for his wife. Vixen smelt the kill and smiled.

"It's lovely, thank you," said Vixen, taking a big bite.

"I wouldn't go that far," said Fox, "but, you know, first principles..."

One of the cubs looked up and stopped suckling.

"What are first principles?" asked the cub.

Fox looked to Vixen who nodded and returned to her meal.

"There are codes on the Charnwood," said Fox, "and maybe on the Charnwood this is more important. However, the first principle for all foxes is that even if there is a tastier meal nearby, if you spot a rat you must hunt that first."

One of the cubs looked confused.

"Isn't that just picking on the Rats?" he said, "You told us last week that bullying was bad."

"There are reasons," said Fox, "you see there are some species of rats that humans keep as pets which are as polite and kind as the day is long, however, they are not the same as Rats in the wild."

"What's different about the wild Rats?" asked another cub.

"Well Rats are like humans. One on their own can be nice, even friendly. But the more of them there are the more aggressive they become and when they swarm, they are a danger to us and everything else. Here on the Charnwood, it can get even worse... Shall mother tell you the story of the Rat invasion of Fayre?"

The cubs all nodded, and Vixen began.

***

A long, long time ago. Long before the war of elves and goblins, long before Kapol-Tok was lost and before humans became so noisy there was

peace on the Charnwood. In these days, of all the folk from other worlds, it was the Fairies who visited most. Those were the days of the Old Queen when Fairies were kind and fair, and both Fairies and Pixies were loved equally in the land of Fayre.

It was in this time that the Rats started making friends of Fairies. Always helping them find the best nectar and flowers and letting them ride on their backs

(Fairies can fly and are very strong, but it's amazing how many of them preferred to let someone else do the hard work.) In time, even the Old Queen grew to love the rats and often had some staying at the palace, they dined on the nicest fruits and were given cloaks of the finest thread.

One day, one of the Rats approached the Old Queen and asked if she and her family could move to Fayre permanently. The Queen agreed and the family were given some land far to the south.

The Queen didn't know, however, that for Rats brothers and sisters could be husbands and wives.

Within a few years the Rats approached the Queen asking for more land. The Queen assented but something about it made her feel uncomfortable. Maybe the rats had not been quite as polite as before. Only a year later the Rats told the Queen they needed more land. They didn't ask, they demanded. The Queen said

she would have to think about it. Other villages closer to the rat-land began complaining that their crops were being stolen. Eventually the Queen had no choice but to send a message demanding that the Rats either abide by their laws or return to Earth. The message got no response.

Eventually the Queen went herself to see what was going on. Some say she took her young daughter with her, and maybe that's why the new Queen went the way she did. Long before they reached what was supposed to be the limit of the rat-land, they found the rats. Long before that they smelt the rats. The lands all around were devastated. Not only were the rich grass pastures devastated, but there was also the stench of uncovered rat poo everywhere. The Rats were swarming, eating everything. They couldn't be spoken to. They couldn't be reasoned with. Some even attacked the Queen's guard.

The result was a five-year war between the Rats and the Fairies. Even we Foxes, never to do

so before and never again, travelled to Fayre. We fought beside the Fairies and Guardians.

Rats breed so quickly that there was an almost never-ending army. Luckily, Fairies and Pixies are practically indestructible by Earth standards. But Rats, once in the mood to fight, would not back down, even to the last one, and even though they were offered, many times, free escort back to Earth, none returned. Restoring the lands they destroyed and removing their filth took decades.

\*\*\*

"And that my little ones, is the reason for our standing orders," said Vixen. "Not only to keep us fed but to save the Charnwood, if not the world. However, at the same time, Rats, even brown Rats, have the right to exist, so we help keep them in check."

"I feel a little sorry for them," said one of the cubs.

"That's okay in here," said Vixen, "but out there? Well... we must eat, and Rats are number one on the menu."

## Chapter Six:
## Moles (and Shrews).

"Never," said Fox, "eat a shrew. Shrews are full of toxins and no good for you; even if you were lucky enough to find one. If they bite you, you will get a nasty sting. They have a horrible smell which is hard to shift. They taste even worse than they smell, and after all that, they have no goodness in them to make it worth eating."

The cubs nodded wisely, though never having seen a shrew they had no idea.

"The same is true for Moles," said Fox, "though you very rarely see them. But Moles are very much the forest's friend."

"Why?" asked Brush, being the most inquisitive cub.

"Well..." answered Fox, "Ask your mother and she will find the right story to explain."

Vixen looked up at Fox and batted her eyelids at him.

"Oh I'll tell them the one about the Brownies and Bracken," said Vixen, "I know you love that one."

Fox looked at her and smiled.

"Okay," he said, and Fox sat with the cubs as Vixen began.

\*\*\*

Long, long ago and on another world, the Brownies lived happy and contented lives. They often visited the Charnwood and still do, even when Kapol-Tok was cut off, they were able to come here through the Thringstone fault.

Brownies are much loved by us Foxes. Especially cubs. For Brownies are made of the stuff of trees and shrubs which we cannot eat and what they eat is no harm to us. They fell in love with the Charnwood for the Rowan berries. Though many birds eat the Rowan berries, and Humans can make a jam out of them if they wish, most of them go to waste. The Brownies make

use of them as they don't grow on Bracken, their home world.

The world of Bracken is made entirely of plant life. No insects, no animals, no fish, no birds, just plants.

Now Brownies love games like hide and seek and so Foxes and cubs love chasing them. Even Guardians play with Brownies and they are extremely friendly and kind.

However there came a time when their world suffered a famine. Their crops were failing, and it was said by some that the soil needed to be brought back to life, regenerated and the best way to do that was with worms.

So worms were introduced to Bracken where no animal (except for visitors) had ever been. It was a resounding success and soon the soil was once more rich and the crops good.

But the worms had no natural predators on Bracken. Soon there was a plague of worms, the fields and forest floors became a sea of wriggling

worms. The Brownies begged the Guardians for help.

The Guardians were quite annoyed as nobody had asked them if introducing worms would be a good idea in the first place. The Brownies didn't say who it was that had suggested it to them. But many believe the new Fairy Queen was behind it and the famine.

The Guardians thought and considered and in the end found some Moles. Now Moles can't talk. But they can understand, and when they heard the Guardians' plan they agreed happily.

You see Moles eat worms. All the time. Constantly. They also keep worms in larders that they make underground. Sometimes with thousands of worms inside. Just one lick from a mole is enough to send a worm to sleep and then the Moles carry them off.

The deal was this: Special wooden larders would be built, and the Moles would travel to Bracken and hunt down the worms. They would

put the worms in the wooden larders (well, boxes) and then bring them back to Earth.

Within a couple of months there wasn't a worm left. The Moles were very happy and returned to Earth with their larders. The Brownies were happy, and the Guardians worked with them to ensure that if they were in trouble again, natural solutions could be found.

\*\*\*

"The lesson," said Fox, "is this. Though we eat worms ourselves when there is nothing better, Moles only eat worms. If not for Moles, birds and many other creatures that eat them, worms could become a plague. So, Moles are friends of the forest and the countryside, whatever Humans may say.

# Chapter Seven:
## Bats.

"Tell us a tale," the cubs all cried. They had just finished their first meal of real food and were feeling a little out of sorts. Though meat was filling it was not as comforting as mother's milk. A few cubs tried to suckle; however, mother was having none of it.

"If you settle down and stop bothering me," said Vixen, "I will tell you of bats."

The cubs all settled down, and Vixen began.

"You will often see and hear bats at night. They fly around and eat insects. They are not birds; they are mammals just like us. They are capable of speech, but few can understand them save the Guardians. Now it can be tempting to jump up and try to catch a bat for dinner, don't bother, they are small and leathery, and you will use more energy trying to catch

them than you will get from eating them. Also, you must be careful, their bones are hollow and just batting them with your paw can hurt them terribly. There are reasons you should not eat them. The Bat communication network is an important part of the Charnwood. In fact, there was a time when it saved many lives."

"Tell us," the cubs cried.

And so, Vixen did.

***

In 1796 a dam was built in the Charnwood, creating the 'Blackbrook Reservoir'. It was built too near the Thringstone fault and in 1799 the Thringstone fault produced an earthquake and the dam burst. Many animals were lost, and some people. The men who built the dam just built it again only stronger. In 1957, only 70 years ago, the Thringstone fault was active again, it cracked the dam. The dam held in our world, but the Thringstone fault is not just a crack in the

Earth, it's a crack in the universe. It was then the cloud-slugs appeared.

*** 

"What are cloud-slugs?" asked a cub, but Vixen carried on.

***

They didn't appear that very night, however it was on that night that a rift opened between their world and ours. It was some months later and there was a heavy fog on the Charnwood. Mists rose off the water of the Blackwood Reservoir, and through the mists came the cloud-slugs, huge as houses, they lumbered about eating the mist as Cows eat grass.

Although the cloud-slugs are peaceful they are dangerous. Animals that touch the slugs can be hurt and even killed.

One of them lumbered into an electricity pylon. (They are big Human metal things) and made it explode. Now the Guardians were far away that night, doing their rounds, and after the

earthquake were keeping clear of the reservoir in case it burst again.

By now it was early April, and the Bats were looking for food after their long winter sleep. The fog is not a danger to Bats as it is to us. Luckily Bats use their ears like we use our noses to see what our eyes cannot. While thick fog may make it harder in some ways, for bats it can help in other ways, making gliding easier they say.

It wasn't long before there were many bats by the water's edge, for that is where the tastiest insects can be found. As soon as the cloud slugs appeared the Bats could see them through their ears. Quick as you like the fastest of them scattered in all directions looking for Guardians. The remaining Bats watched the cloud-slugs from every angle, so when at last the Guardians appeared they could give a full report. They spotted the different calls that the cloud-slugs made to each other, too high or low for Humans to hear. It was through the Bat reports that the Guardians were able to discover that certain sounds kept the cloud slugs from advancing.

Bats

Alas not until one had hit the pylon. These days, whenever the cloud-slugs come through the Guardians are ready for them and stop them harming any of the creatures of the Charnwood. And for that we must thank the Bats. There have

been other times the Bats have warned of visitors from other realms and for that reason if not for many others, we should leave them in peace.

***

The Cubs yawned and snuggled up to their mum's side.

"We're very lucky to live on the Charnwood," said one of the cubs.

"Yes," said Vixen, "we are."

THE END

Printed in Dunstable, United Kingdom